Copyright © by Lon S. Safko

All rights reserved. No part of this book may be used or reproduced by any means, graphic, electronic, or mechanical, including photocopying, recording, taping or by any information storage retrieval system without the written permission of the publisher except in the case of brief quotations embodied in critical articles and reviews.

Printed in the United States of America

This book was created using 100% recycled electrons

No animals were harmed in the making of this book

This book is dolphin safe

Fusion: 2020 Marketing
Everything You Need To Know

As many of you know, I am the author of the bestselling book, The Social Media Bible, and my newest bestseller is called The Fusion Marketing Bible. Fusion Marketing is about "What's next", it's what comes after social media. Fusion Marketing is actually an entirely new form of marketing.

I discovered Fusion Marketing as a result of constantly being asked in interviews "So, what comes after social media?" I would think to myself, "Social media has change the way the world markets, sells, and communicates forever. And, it has caused us to change at speeds we have never seen before with technology" and you want to know what's next?

I decided to take that question on as a personal challenge. I asked myself, "Where will marketing and sales organizations be in say, five years? How will we be treating traditional, digital, and social media marketing? That's when I realized that Traditional Marketing + Digital Marketing* + Social Media Marketing = Fusion Marketing!

I realized that even now, if you are calling yourself a "Social Media Expert" then you're announcing to the world that you have been left behind. If you're an expert in Facebook and Twitter, then you're trying to build an entire marketing strategy restricted to using only one or two tools from all of the marketing tools available today. And, the reason we aren't seeing the ROI from social media is, Facebook is not a strategy. Twitter is not a strategy. LinkedIn is not a strategy. They are only tools. We'll get to what is a strategy later.

If you're still stuck looking at social media as a stand alone marketing technology, then you've been left behind. Today the term V.P. Social Media Marketing sounds normal, but it is already as obsolete as V.P. of Billboards. The first companies that recognize that social media marketing is only one set of marketing tools out of many, will be ahead of the curve.

Fusion Marketing is the next generation of marketing that brings all of our 6,000 years of traditional "push" or "monolog" marketing, the exciting digital marketing tools* of the Internet, and social media "two-way communication" or "dialog" marketing and fully integrates them into one seamless toolset that will accomplish every objective you set at no additional cost to you or your company!

*Digital marketing tools are different from social media as they don't imply two-way communication. Social media tools such as Facebook, Twitter, LinkedIn, and others imply a post and a response. Digital tools do not. Examples of digital tools as SEO (Search Engine Optimization), SEM (Search Engine Marketing), RSS (Really Simply Syndication) and eCommerce. These are all necessary for marketing and aid in your being found on the Internet, but doesn't imply two-way communication.

Fusion Marketing is such a totally new concept of "Fusing" all of your marketing tools that it has been accepted by the United States Patent & Trademark Office as "Patent Pending".

As part of the Fusion Marketing concept, I also invented a tool to help you implement your Fusion Marketing Plan called the Safko Wheel. You can get this development tool for free with the purchase of The Fusion Marketing Bible book or you can just make one from scratch.

This article is about how Fusion Marketing and the Safko Wheel works, and how you can use these tools to discover hidden ROI opportunities in your marketing without spending a cent more. Fusion Marketing is a 12 Step process and here's how it works.

(Trust me... It's fun and it really works!)

Fusion Marketing & The Safko Wheel
A 12 Step Process

The Set Up

Get the book / Wheel or just make one. Cut out or create the 20 "Traditional Tool" cards and the 20 "Digital / Social Media Tool" cards and at least one Wheel (a 20 pointed starburst). Place the 20 Traditional Tool cards around the Wheel as you see below.

Traditional Tool Analysis

Step 1 – Select Your Traditional Tools

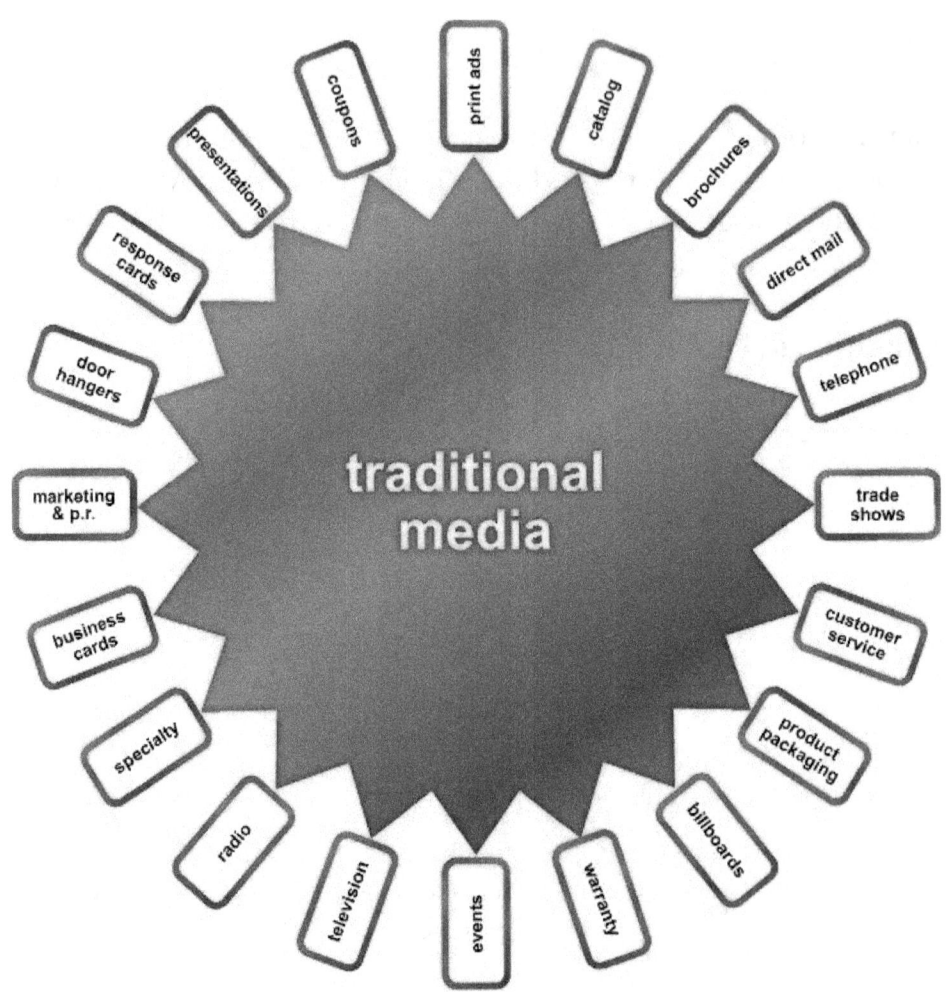

Step 1a - Place Traditional Tools Around Safko Wheel

Select the Traditional Marketing Tools you used last year and any Tools you think you will use this year and remove the remaining Tools from around the Wheel. Your wheel might look something like this Wheel below.

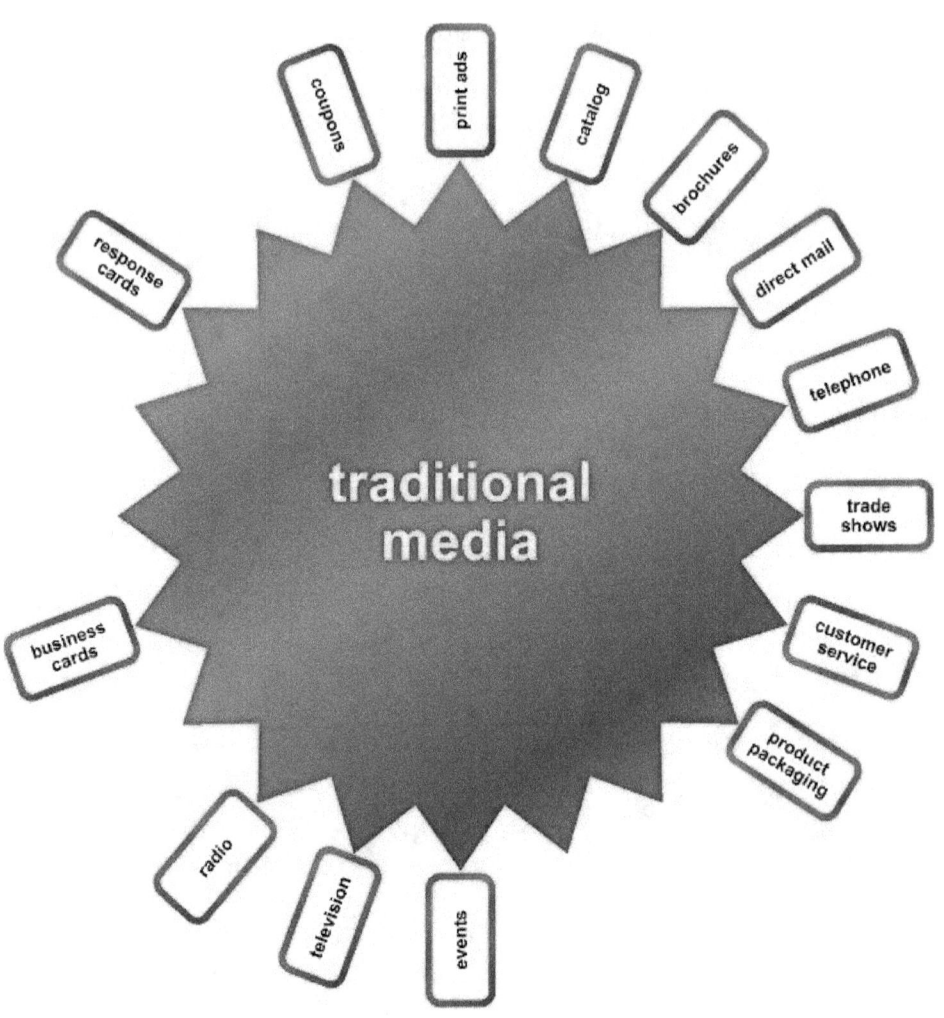

Step 1b - Remove The Traditional Tools You Didn't Use Last Year

Step 2 – Perform Fusion Marketing (Traditional)
Fusion Marketing is about "fusing" all your marketing Tools together to create a custom master Toolset and discovering new marketing opportunities.

a) Select & Study First Tool
Select one Tool from the Wheel. Study that Tool for a moment to understand how it really works. For example, at first I thought the business card Tool had the worst ROI of any Tool on the Wheel. I can't remember every making a sale from a business card; however, when I thought about it, I realized that a business card represents a personal relationship. We touched each other (legally), with a handshake. Business cards represent a relationship you can't create through either Traditional or Social Media marketing; it's very personal.

b) Select & Study Your Second Tool
Then, randomly select a second Tool from the Wheel and study it. See what you can find in that Tools that will help you "Fuse" with your prospects and customers. An example would be the coupon Tool. How does my customer use my coupon? What are they thinking? Do they have any questions?

c) The First Fusion Connection
Now, Fuse Tool 1 with Tool 2. Using the example above How can I Fuse business cards and coupons? Ask yourself "How can they work together?" At first you will not see any logical Connection. It doesn't seem to make sense to Fuse to unrelated Tools. Keep trying, you'll see the Connection.

What if you put a coupon on the back of your business card? Nearly everyone's business card is blank on the back. Why? That's important marketing real estate! You would never leave a blank page on a brochure... 10 seconds of dead air on the radio... Then why is your business card back... blank?

We also know that business cards represent a strong interaction, face-to-face, relationship and coupons are a good way to convert a prospect into a customer. Would putting a coupon on your business card make a customer more likely to purchase while holding and viewing your card and remembering meeting and spending time with you? Of course it would!

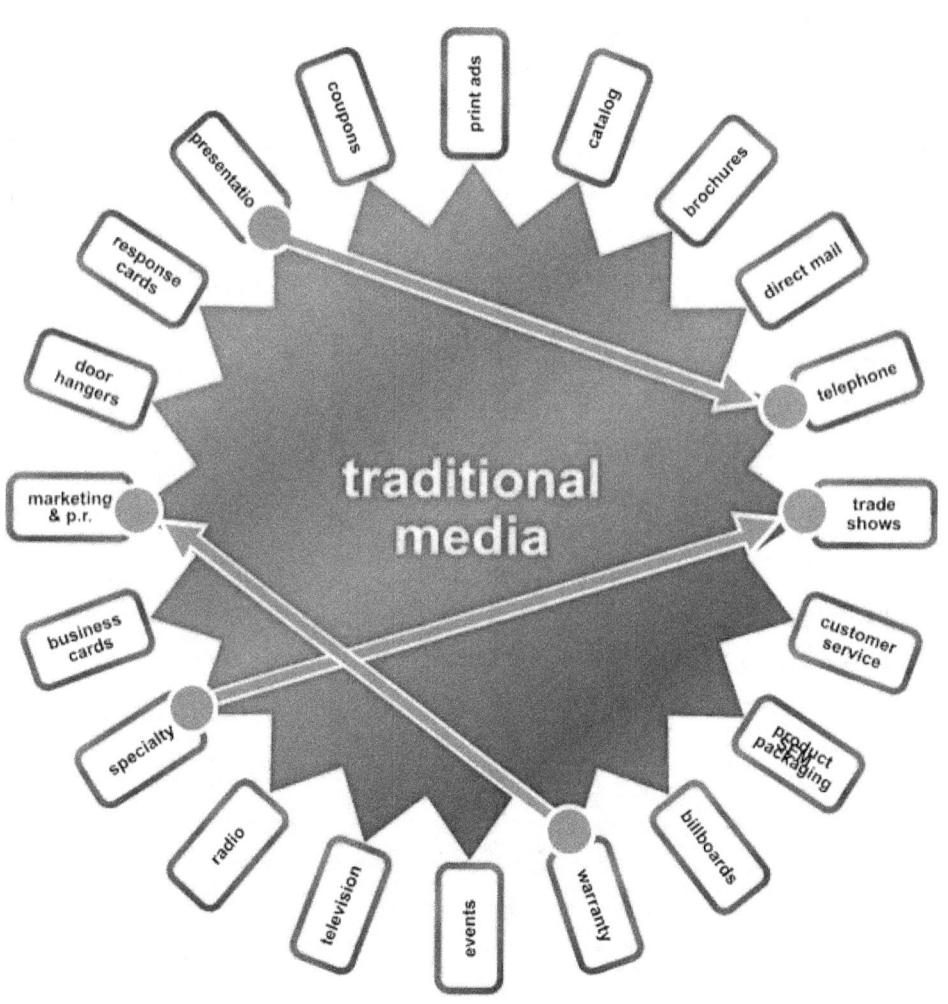

Step 2c - Make Fusion Connections With Random Tools

Let's look at another Fusion Connection. What if you put the information about your next trade show on the back of your business cards with a QR Barcode that led to a web page or video that said, "If you are in Atlanta on May 23, stop by booth 2103 for a demo and free gift!". Would that generate more traffic? Of course it would.

Business cards are really cheap and now, they are all print on demand. Why not change out your cards every month with the latest promotion on the back of each? If everyone in your company were instructed to hand out business cards to everyone they met, how many cards (promotion pieces), could be handed out each month? And, at the cost of a business card!

d) Reverse Fusion Connections

Now that you can see how to use the Safko Wheel to make one way Fusion Connections from Tool 1 to Tool 2, let's make Reverse Fusion Connections. Start with the first Toolset (Tools 1 and 2) and "Reverse" the Connection to identify additional opportunities. Try it!

What if you Fused the coupon Tool to the business card Tool and put your personal contact information on your coupon, or put a QR Barcode on your coupon that lead to a video of you, reintroducing yourself and asking the card / coupon holder to give you a call? Would that type of personal message increase leads and sales? Yes, it would...

What if you had a real "person", someone that a prospect could speak with, an individual who represented your company with their personal contact information on your coupon? Would that make a prospect more likely to exercise that coupon and convert from a prospect to a customer? Of course it would!

This creates a personal relationship between you and the buyer. Relationships lead to trust. Trust leads to sales. See LinkedIn article "Trust Sells" (http://linkd.in/1q0F8nL)

e) Multiple Fusion Connections
Now that you have made Connections and Reverse Connections, let's make multiple Fusion Connections. Keep Tool 1, move around the Wheel Fusing that Tool to each, different Tool on the Wheel, one at a time, and discover all the new opportunities hidden in your existing marketing. At first you might not see how they connect, but they will. Give it a chance. Write these ideas down!

f) Reverse New Fusion Connections
Now, reverse each Fusion Connection you make to find more opportunity!

g) Repeat The Fusion Connection Process
When you have completed Fusing your Tool 1 with all of the other Tools, select the another Tool and repeat this whole process again. Move around the Wheel and make Fusion Connections one-way with each new Tool, then reverse each connection!

How many different opportunities can you discover by looking at your Traditional media in this way? The Fusion Marketing way? And, you are already doing it so all these new opportunities came at no extra cost!

Digital Tool Analysis
Step 3 – The Trinity of Social Media

In my books I talk about The Trinity of Social Media; Blogging, Micro-blogging (Twitter), and Social Networks. With only these three Tools, you can accomplish about 90% of the total success Social Media has to offer.

a) Clear the Wheel and save your chosen Traditional Tool cards aside. Place the three "Trinity" cards around the Wheel. Add in other Digital / Social Media Marketing Tools that you think are important to your over all marketing strategy; e.g.: SEO (Search Engine Optimization), SEM (Search Engine Marketing), RSS (Really Simple Syndication), Facebook (social networks), YouTube (video sharing), Email, etc. If you aren't familiar with all 20 major Social Media categories, read The Social Media Bible.

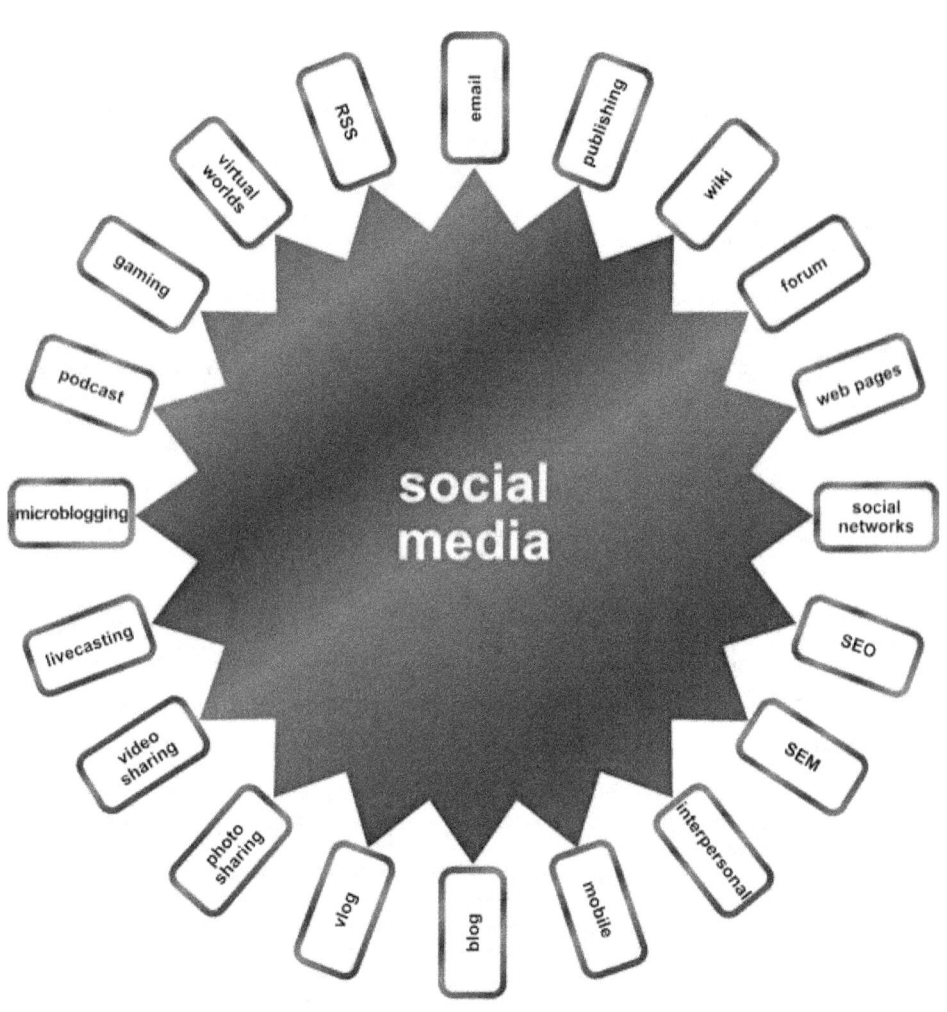

Step 3a - Digital / Social Media Marketing Wheel

Step 4 – Perform Digital / Social Fusion Marketing
Refer to Step 2 above and repeat the processes of Fusing all of your Digital / Social Media Tools together to discover even more new opportunities. How many can you identify?

TraDigital Tool Analysis

Step 5 – Create A TraDigital Toolset
Now is the time combine the chosen Traditional Marketing Tools with the chosen Digital / Social Media Marketing Tools by placing them around the Wheel to create one custom, TraDigital Toolset (Traditional + Digital = TraDigital). You can start making all of the Fusion Connections we made above, but...

Step 6 – Perform The Cost of Customer Acquisition (COCA)
You will quickly see that there are just too many possible connections. None of us have the time or resources to pursue all those hidden, but valuable opportunities. With only the 20 Top Traditional and the 20 Top Digital / Social Media Tools, there are $8.15 \times 10(47)$ or 8 with 47 zeros after it, combinations. We will have to scale this down somehow that makes sense.

a) To scale this down, we will perform the Cost of Customer Acquisition on each Tool (marketing campaign). Start by listing all of the Traditional campaigns you performed last year on a whiteboard, yellow-pad, or spreadsheet. List every expense, be sure to include all of your overhead. Total the columns for those expenses. While this should include everyone's hourly wage, payroll burden (usually 32% for vacation, holidays, sick days, and payroll taxes), and other overhead, you can keep it simple if you wish. The more accurate the numbers in, the better the results out.

b) Estimate the number of new customers each campaign generated and write them at the bottom of the campaign columns. Finally, divide the total expense for each of the campaigns by the number of new customers it generated. This is your Cost Of Customer Acquisition, (COCA).

You don't know how many new customers each campaign generated... Then you need to measure! That's another article. If you have been measuring, these numbers will surprise you, some in a good way and some will cause you shock. This is the only step in the Fusion Marketing process that requires a little work. The rest is fun!

Step 7 – Eliminate and Prioritize
a) Here's where you eliminate campaigns that were ineffective; the ones with the poorest ROI or the worst COCA will be eliminated. Keep doing what's working, stop doing what's not. This will provide new human and financial resources that we can use later on Tools that actually work. Be sure add in any new Tools (cards) you wish to incorporate this year strategy.

I want you to stop doing marketing by accident and begin doing your marketing deliberately.

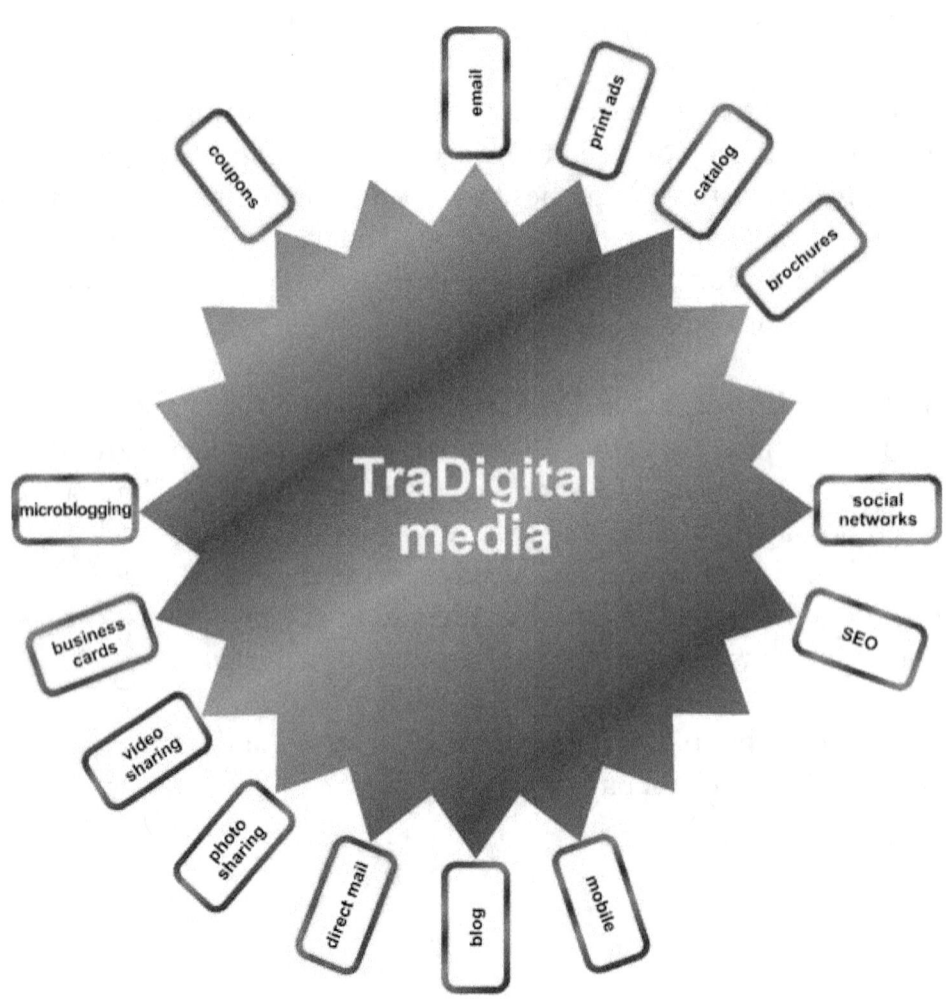

Step 7b - Digital / Social Media TraDigital Marketing Wheel

Fusion Marketing

Step 8 – Perform Fusion Marketing

At this stage, you now have a fully custom set of marketing Tools design by you for you. This process has eliminated all of the Traditional marketing tools you were using, which had little or bad ROI. You selected Digital / Social Media Tools that you know will work for you and you alone. This TraDigital Toolset is custom designed by you, for your company.

a) Again, refer to Step 2 above for Fusing and Reverse Fusing these Tools and experience the process of Fusing all of your Tools together to discover dozens of new opportunities.

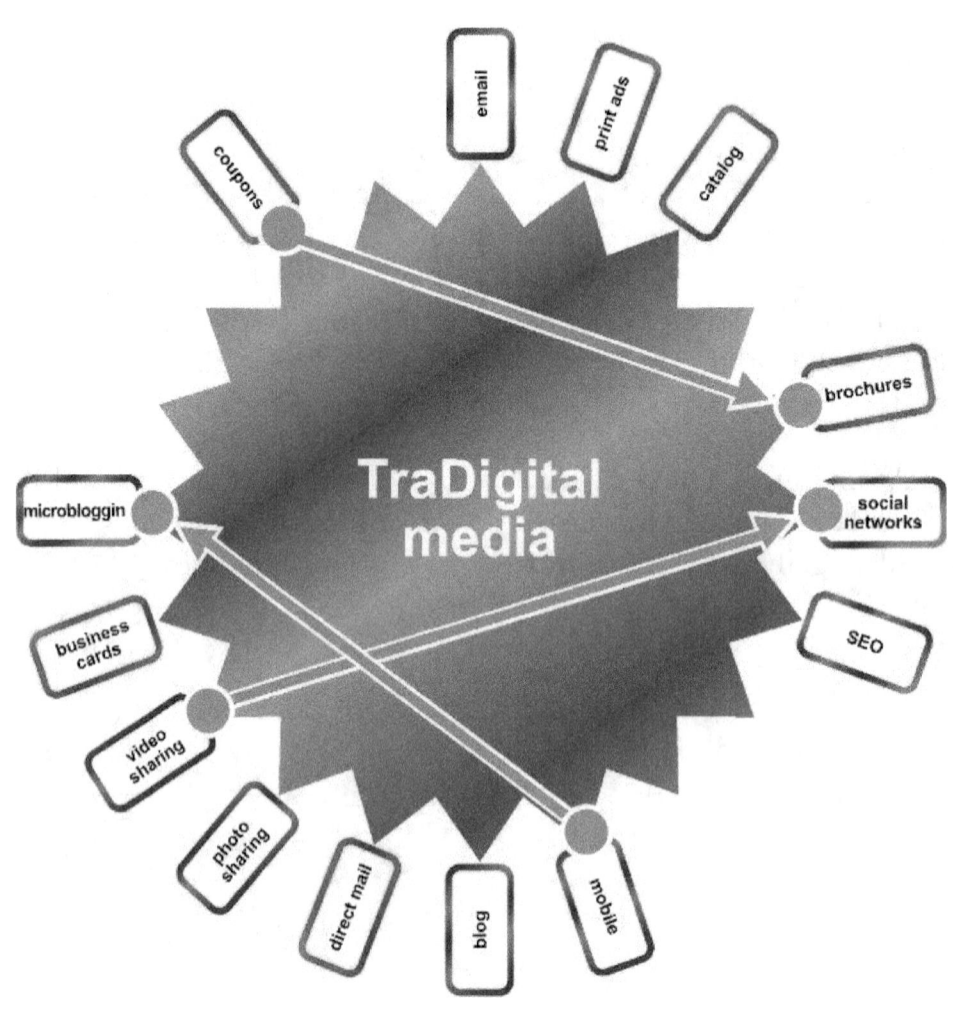

Step 8a - TraDigital Marketing Wheel Connections

Here is an actual example of what I found when Fusing and Reverse Fusing my custom Tools:

Second Life and Web Pages

Before you yell "What's wrong with the guy?! Doesn't he know Second Life crashed and burned in 2015? Where's he been?"

I know, but you have to admit that the two major new and unexplored frontiers in marketing is Augmented Reality and Virtual Reality. Agree? Then, have you spent 1,000 hours or more in developing in a virtual world? I have. Is there yet, a better more sophisticated place that you can develop, for free?

I didn't think so. Please, follow my lead here.

I chose two random Tools and looked at how they could Connect. I first chose web pages and Second Life (www.SecondLife.com). For those of you who aren't familiar with Second Life, it's an on-line three-dimensional world that people use to meet other people, do business, teach, entertain, and just explore the virtual world. I, like many others, use Second Life for business.

My Virtual Property In Second Life

My Second Life Virtual Stores

I have two "real" stores on my virtual property In Second Life where I sell "Three-Dimensional Internet Advertising", which I own three U.S. Patents on and my Educational CD's, DVD, and books. I also hold international meetings and interviews and teach virtual classes for universities around the world. And, I even do PowerPoint presentations to groups of avatars (students).

I chose these two Tools, web sites and Second Life to start with, because I felt that had the lowest ROI and the least in common. Second Life is what they call a "thin client" or small app (software) that runs on your computer and we all know how web pages work.

By using the Safko Wheel and Fusing these two "un-connectable" Tools, I suddenly realized, that on every one of my web sites, any mention of my participation of Second Life, was missing. Nowhere did they say that I am marketing in Second Life. I never would have thought to connect these two unrelated marketing Tools.

VISIT LON IN SECOND LIFE

My Second Life Avatar

So, I went to my virtual office in Second Life, grabbed a screen capture of my avatar, and placed the image along with a link back to SecondLife on my web sites. Within 24 hours, I saw a 400% increase in my visitors in Second Life!

There were 16.5 million members on Second Life, many of whom visit my web sites, but didn't know I was on SL. Now I and driving a significant share of those members from my web site to my virtual store in my virtual world.

The next task was the Fusing the Reverse Connection by promoting my web sites within Second Life. So, I created a large framed image that I placed on the wall in my virtual store that read "Mention Second Life with Your Paid Order And Receive A Free $50 DVD!" Guess what? I saw a 180% increase in traffic in my e-commerce web store in the first 24 hours. This is when I knew Fusion Marketing really works!

Fusing Second Life To My Web Pages

Strategy, Objective, Tool, and Tactic Development

Step 9 – Defining Strategy, Objectives, Tactics, & Tools

In this step I define Strategy, Objectives, Tactics, & Tools and create everything you will need to build a successful Fusion Marketing Plan. Strategy = Objectives + Tools + Tactics.

You might think you know the definition of strategy, but you might not. Go ahead and take a moment to define "strategy" in your head... Really... I'll wait... Not so easy is it?

It's because a Strategy isn't a thing. Strategy is the compilation of your Objectives, Tools, and Tactics. It's an outcome, not a single item. It's like the word "synergy". Synergy is where the whole is greater than the sum of its parts. Stay with me here...

Create Objectives
a) Let's begin by creating Objectives, not goals. They're not the same. A goal is a value you place on the outcome of a particular Tactic in order to measure and compare its effectiveness.

We will create 5 Objectives. An Objective is what you want your marketing to accomplish. At the end of the year, quarter, or campaign, what do you want your marketing to achieve, such as; "increase email list", "drive more attendance to presentations", "perform more webinars", or "drive more traffic to my e-commerce store". The "amount" of additional traffic is defined by your goal.

These are the ones I created for my first Fusion Marketing Plan, Create yours and write then down. Create five, no more as you will not have the resources to execute all of the great ideas that you will discover.

b) Place the first Objective you created in the center of your custom Safko TraDigital Wheel. As an example, I will use "Build Email List", as I know the value of email marketing.

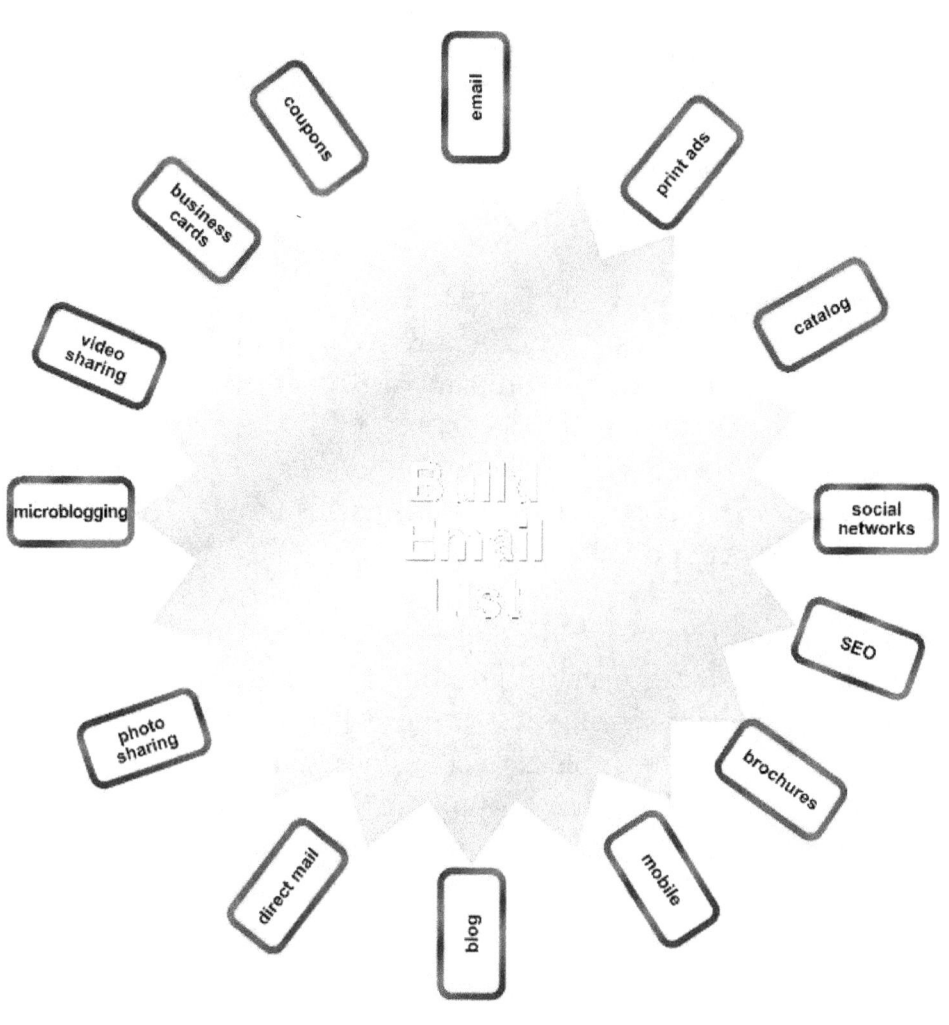

Step 9b - The Safko Strategy Wheel - Objective & Tools

Step 10 – Develop All Of Your Tactics

It's time to work the Wheel now that yo0u have placed one of your Objectives you created in the center of the Wheel.

a) Select each Tool, one at a time, and ask, "How can I use this Tools to achieve that Objective?"

My example question would be, "How can I use 'business cards' to increase my email list?" My answer: "What if I put a QR Barcode on the back of my company cards that lead the holder directly to my email sign up page." Or, "a QR Code to a video explaining the benefits of receiving your emails?" Or, "to a web address that offered a white paper or other fish food?" All good ideas? Write them down!

b) Move around the Wheel Fusing each Tool to that one Objective. These Connections are your Tactics. Try making multiple connections; using two or more Tools to Connect to the Objective as in the example above; business cards, QR bar codes, and video sharing. Continue around the Wheel using every Tools. Record every Tactic. Repeat this process with the remaining Objectives until you have fully developed all of the Tactics for all five of your Objectives.

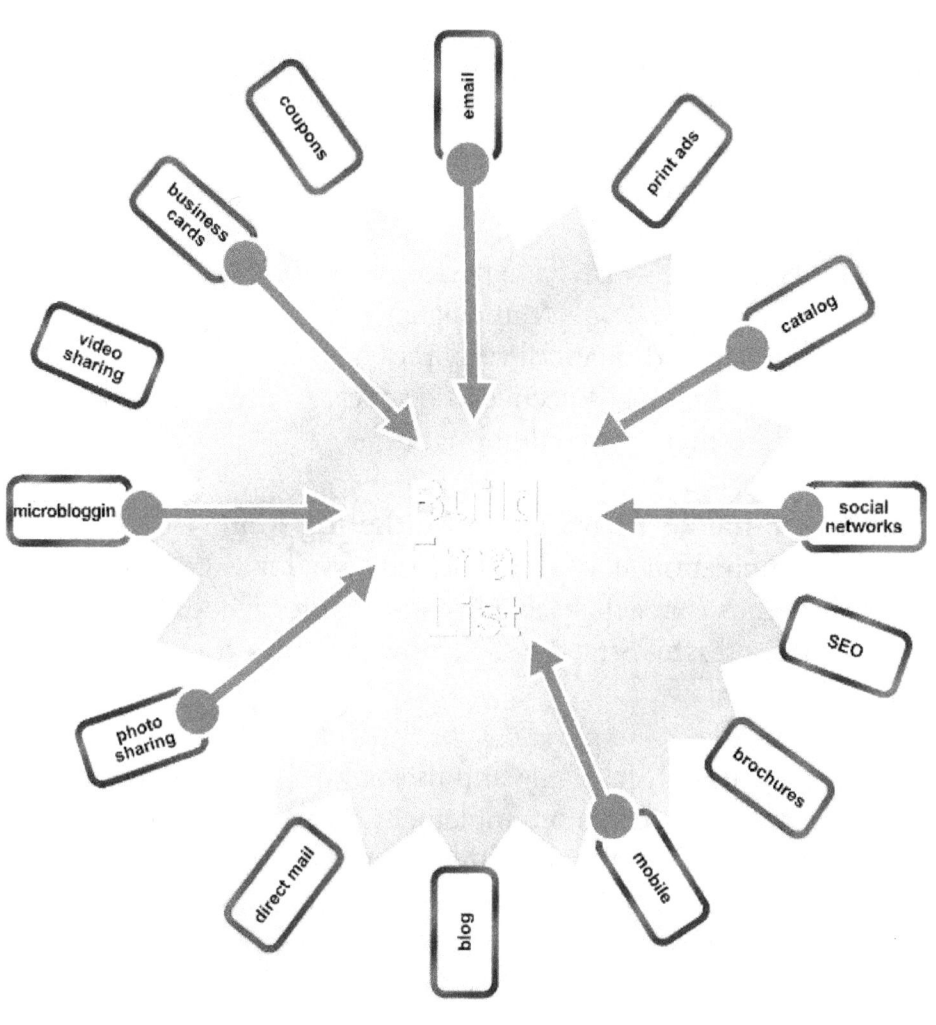

Step 10b - The Safko Strategy Wheel - Objectives, Tools, & Tactics

Step 11 – Prioritize Your Tactics

a) The next step is prioritizing each Tactic you recorded for each Objective, because you can't do everything. If you chose only 20 custom Tools and created 5 Objectives, you would discover more than 100 sound executable Tactics that you know will work.

Remember, now that you have performed your COCA in Step 6, and have eliminated Tools (campaigns) with a poor ROI, you now have the human and financial resources, which can be applied to accomplish additional Objectives / Tactics. And you are doing all this anyway so there is no additional expense!

Step 12 – Finalize Your Fusion Marketing Plan

It's the combination all of the above custom Tools generating custom Tactics for each selected custom Objective that becomes your final successful Strategy. This now becomes your new Fusion Marketing Plan!

By utilizing Fusion Marketing and the Safko Wheel process you will only spend resources on implementing your most effective Tactics, on the most effective Objectives, using the most effective Traditional Marketing Tools, combined with the most effective Digital Marketing Tools, to develop the most effective Strategy!

That's it! Fusion Marketing is a process that systematically encourages you to look at all of your marketing in a completely different way to identify hidden opportunities to increase your ROI without spending any additional money.

Isn't this every marketer's dream? To see greater ROI across every category of marketing with less cost?

EXECUTE WITH SUCCESS!

For the complete story and many more way to use Fusion Marketing, go to Amazon and purchase "The Fusion Marketing Bible".

For more information and everything you ever wanted to know about social media, go to Amazon and purchase "The Social Media Bible".

For more information about the author, please visit:

www.LonSafko.com

www.ingramcontent.com/pod-product-compliance
Lightning Source LLC
Chambersburg PA
CBHW050035230526
45470CB00003B/1291